SHERMAN
in action

by Bruce Culver

illustrated by Don Greer

 squadron/signal publications

"Battling Bitch", an M4A1 of the U.S. 7th Armored Division's 31st Tank Battalion chasing the retreating Germans across the plains of Central France. Seen here near Chartres in August 1944, it still carries the Cullin Hedgerow Device installed during the Normandy Campaign.

ISBN 0-89747-049-4

also by Bruce Culver

Panther in Action
PzKpfw IV in Action
Sturmgeschutz in Action
Panzer Colors with Bill Murphy

Photo Credits
US Army

Editor's Note

This book is the first of a new series from Squadron/Signal Publications on U.S. Armor. Because of the great amount of material available, this first book is limited to the M4 Sherman gun-armed tanks that saw combat service with U.S. forces. The M3 medium tanks, Lend-Lease M4's used by other nations, and all special-purpose or modified Shermans - bulldozer tanks, flamethrowers, rocket launchers, wading tanks, TRV's, etc. - will be covered in a companion volume. Other books are being projected to cover the full range of American combat vehicles used in World War II.

Vehicles of the 752nd Tank Battalion, attached to the Fifth Army, wait in the Plaza Emanuel, Bologna, Italy near the end of the war. Even at this late date, 21 April 1945, there is an ancient early production M4 [4th from the right, front row] still retaining its direct vision slots in the glacis plate. Note the variety of vehicles, including M5A1 light tanks and M18 tank destroyers, and the difference in crew stowage and fitting details.

Sherman Development

The M4 Sherman tank is one of the most famous and significant armored vehicles ever built. It was constructed in greater numbers than any other tank, and examples are still in second-line service in several parts of the world. Maligned by some for its faults, glorified by others because of its service successes, the M4 series, perhaps more than any other vehicle, symbolized the basic differences in philosophy between the United States and her enemies in World War II: rugged, unsophisticated, perfectly suited for mass production, the Sherman family eventually numbered over 55,000 vehicles, well over twice the number of tanks built by Germany from 1939-1945. Its numbers, reliability, and ease of handling and maintenance were the great strengths of the M4 family, and the basic reasons for its success as a combat tank.

Sherman tank development goes back directly to the T5 medium tank built by Rock Island arsenal in 1938. Designed to use suspension components and power train designs from then-current light tanks, the T5 and its developments, the M2 and M2A1 medium tanks, influenced the mechanical layout and basic design of the progenitor of the M4 series: the M3 medium. The M3 resulted from new specifications drawn up when it became obvious that the M2/M2A1 mediums would be obsolete before they were built. Since the Germans were mounting 7.5cm guns in the PzKpfw IV and 5cm guns in the PzKpfw III, Ordnance, and the newly created Armored Force of the U.S. Army, stressed the importance of mounting a 75mm gun in a more heavily armored tank.

Further development of the T5 pilot series resulted in the M3 medium tank in early 1941. The M3 was accepted as an interim type only, pending the development of a turret mounting 75mm gun with full traverse. The M3s sponson-mounted 75mm M2 had limited traverse and prevented use of full hull-down positions, but its armor-piercing capabilities and ability to fire HE ammunition were of great value in North Africa.

In 1940 development of a full-traversing turret mount continued, and in April 1941 five provisional configurations were presented to the Army, which chose the simplest for development of the new medium tank. In May 1941 a wooden mockup was approved pending changes, and in September the first pilot model, the T6 medium tank, was delivered to Aberdeen Proving Ground. After completing tests successfully, the T6 was standardized for production as the Medium Tank, M4, in October 1941. Although M3 medium production had been underway only a few months, the M4 production plan called for a gradual phaseout of M3 production with replacement by the newer design.

The M4 medium tank pilot model had a cast "turtleback" hull with side access doors, and a round cast turret mounting a 75mm M2, L/31 gun. The MG cupola on top of the turret, characteristic of M3 Lees, was removed and a much lower split hatch ring was substituted. Because of the difficulty expected in meeting the projected production requirements (at one point set at 2,000 vehicles per month), a simple box-shaped welded hull was adopted for those manufacturers who had no facilities or experience in the casting of armor steel components as large as the Sherman hull. As a result, the welded hull was standardized in October 1941 as the M4 medium, and the cast hull model similar to the prototype was standardized in December 1941 as the M4A1. The hull side doors were eliminated, and other minor changes made before production got underway.

The prototype and M4 and M4A1 models were designed to use the Contintental radial, an aircraft engine. While the adapting of aircraft engines was a tested and successful method of powering tanks, it was realized that with expanded production of both tanks and aircraft, the supply would soon be insufficient. Thus, alternate powerplant installations were adopted, and each of these was given a new model designation. The M4A2, standardized in December 1941, had a welded hull similar to the M4 but was powered by two GMC 6-71 diesel engines. This variant was not used in action by U.S. troops, though it was issued to Allied forces under Lend-Lease. The M4A3, standardized in January 1942, used the new Ford GAA V-8 tank engine - which originally had been a 12 cylinder design for aircraft use. The M4A3 became one of the most important U.S. versions of the Sherman, and was the model standardized after the war, eventually serving in the Korean conflict as well. The M4A4, standardized in February 1942, used the Chrysler "multibank" engine, which was essentially five 6-cylinder automobile engines arranged around a common shaft. Though this engine proved to be quite reliable, its complexity raised questions about its serviceability, and the M4A4 was the first version phased out of production. Most M4A4s were supplied to Britain. The M4A5 was the U.S. "paper" designation for the Canadian-built "Ram" tanks, and the M4A6 was a limited production type using an RD-1820 air-cooled radial diesel, never used in action. Excluding the "M4A5" Rams, total M4 Sherman production came to over 46,900 tanks.

With combat experience derived from the M3 medium and the earlier models of the M4, many thousands of engineering changes were made in the design and layout of the Sherman variants. More reliable mechanical components, better armor protection, improved fire prevention measures, better armament, sights, and suspensions all helped to make the final models of the Sherman vastly superior fighting vehicles than the first models that faced Rommel's Afrika Korps in the Fall of 1942. It should also be understood that some of the admitted faults of the early Shermans were the result of American inexperience in designing combat vehicles and the need to use many components from the M3 medium.

The real key to the controversy over how "good" the Sherman was can be found in the official Army armor doctrine of the WWII period. Essentially, this was that tanks were to be used as a maneuvering force in support of infantry offensive operations, and were to serve as mobile fire support to overcome enemy strong points. It was not the function of the Armored Force tanks to engage and destroy enemy armor - this was the mission of the Tank Destroyer Command. Thus, there was real resistance in many official circles to attempts by Ordnance to improve the Sherman (at least, in terms of firepower), or to introduce newer tanks like the Pershing. These decisions were made in good faith for reasons of established doctrine, but there is no denying that in some situations when U.S. tanks were forced to fight against numbers of good enemy tanks, like the Panther and Tiger, many Shermans and crews were lost because the antitank capabilities of their vehicles had deliberately been subordinated to that of the Tank Destroyers, even to reserving the "hottest" 76mm ammunition for the TD's. Perhaps the wonder is not that the M4 succeeded in spite of its early problems, but that, given the restrictions imposed by circumstances, it was as good as it was. At the time of its first service evaluations in early 1942, the M4 Sherman was easily one of the best all-round tanks in the world.

M4 Characteristics

The M4 medium tank, the first model standardized for production, was in fact the third type to go into production. Five separate plants built the M4, deliveries beginning in July 1942. The final 75mm M4s were delivered in January 1944, and total production was 6,748 gun tanks. All M4s were powered by a single Wright-built R-975-C1 9-cylinder radial engine, driving the vehicle through a 5-speed manual synchromesh transmission and final drive located in the nose. The height of the engine and angled propeller shaft resulted in the typical rather high and angular M4 hull. The simple, box-like hull with vertical sides was designed for rapid production, and the vertical sides were dictated by the width limitations on the vehicle and by the large 69" turret ring. Full length sponsons over the tracks were needed to provide enough clearance for the turret ring, and these were used for ammunition and equipment stowage. The one-piece cast turret had a full turret basket and carried a 75mm M3, L/40 and a .30 M1919A4 LMG as a coaxial gun in the Combination Mount M34. This provided an external mantlet for the main gun only, and the coaxial gun was unprotected, the fixed mantlet having a slot to allow the MG to elevate with the main armament.

The crew consisted of 5 men: the driver and assistant driver/bow gunner in the hull, and the commander, gunner, and loader in the turret. The gunner was in the right front part of the turret with the commander behind him, and the loader was on the left. Hatches were provided for the two hull positions and in the commander's position, although emergency exists for the 3 men in the turret were a problem.

Very early M4s retained the M3 medium tank bogie with the return roller mounted over the bogie casing. The transmission cover in front was a 3-piece design bolted together. The hatches for the driver and assistant driver were in box extensions in the 60° inclined glacis plate and had direct vision slots with armor visors in front. Usually, a plain rubber block track was used. In the rear, double access doors, held closed by a strap bolted to the hull rear plate, were flanked by a pair of air cleaners. The air cleaners were of two patterns - rounded can shape, and a more common box-section type. The engine deck was of solid plates, with a large access hatch hinged behind an armored air intake cowl set beneath the turret rear. Pioneer tools were carried on the engine deck and large vehicle maintenance tools were carried on the rear plate.

As production proceeded, improvements were constantly being made. The M3 bogies were replaced by the typical M4 Vertical Volute Spring Suspension bogie (VVSS) with a trailing return roller and a metal track support skid over the bogie casing, which was deeper than that used on the M3 to accomodate the larger springs used on the M4. The direct vision slots were removed and fixed periscopes added in front of the hull hatches. The 3-piece transmission housing was replaced by a stronger one-piece casting, and the M34 gun mount was replaced by the M34A1 mount, which had a full-width moving external mantlet which provided protection for the coaxial machine gun. Some vehicles with the M34 mount had a moveable armor shield fitted to the coaxial MG to protect the slot in the fixed mantlet. Problems with ammunition fires led to the development of applique armor, 1" thick plates which were welded over the three sponson ammo bins, and also in front of the driver's and assistant driver's hatch boxes to improve the frontal protection. Applique armor was also usually fitted over the gunner's position in the turret. In order to conserve rubber, two designs of steel track were used, and a rubber block with a raised chevron pattern also appeared. By mid-1943, many of the original deficiencies had been alleviated and the Sherman was proving itself a competent combat vehicle.

Early M4, 1942 Production, 75mm

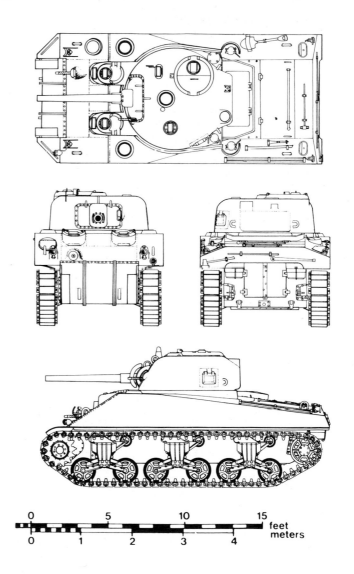

```
0        5        10        15
|_____|_____|_____|____ feet
0    1    2    3    4         meters
```

1:76 th scale (4 mm:1 foot)

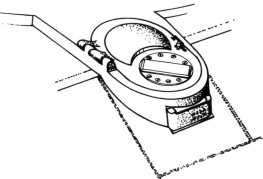

[Right] This early M4 of the 755th Tank Battalion shows the details of the earlier welded hull. It has the three-piece transmission cover, direct vision slots.

Direct Vision Slot

Another early M4 passes through the ruins of Pianoro, Italy, on 20 April 1945. While many early vehicles were remanufactured or field-modified with later features, many old tanks such as this soldiered on to the end of the war in the same configuration in which they were built.

This M4 of the headquarters section of the 59th Field Artillery Battalion was set afire by an artillery strike near Cassino, Italy. Note the sandshields, vision slots and 3-piece transmission cover. The unit symbol of a letter and three colored bars was widely used in Italy and Southern France.

A camouflaged M4 of the 1st Armored Divsion passes through Paganico, Italy in June, 1944. This tank has the redesigned drivers' positions with additional periscopes in front of the hatches, and no vision slots and the M34A1 gun mount with the full width external mantlet.

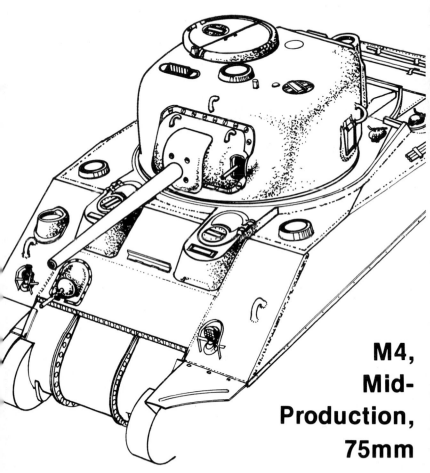

M4, Mid-Production, 75mm

M4 tanks of the 755th Tank Battalion, used as mobile artillery, fire on enemy positions in the Pietramala area of Italy, January 1944. The vehicle on the left has applique armor on the turret, while the M4 in the foreground has an interesting stowage bin extension on the engine deck. Just behind this tank is a pile of cardboard shell tubes used to ship the 75mm ammunition.

This M4 was bogged down in a marsh created when the Germans diverted the Rapido River near Cassino; the river washed out roads and flooded part of the Cassino valley. Note the partial sandshields, round air cleaners and crudely overpainted turret star.

U.S. M4s fire in support of an attack by Moroccan and Algerian troops on Castelforte, Italy, 12 May 1944. The hull side star of "BELLE OF LITTLE ROCK" has been covered with a wash of mud or thin paint to subdue it. Note the casting flaws in the side of the turret.

Standard "Box Type" Air Cleaner

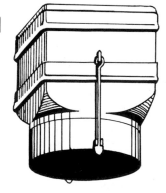

M4's of the 1st Armored Division are seen parked in a valley near Mt. Valbura, Italy, 15 April 1945. The second vehicle from the right has the round pattern air cleaners in the rear; the tank at far right has the more common box-section air cleaners. Each crew has devised its own method to stow the extra equipment U.S. units invariably collected.

This oblique view of an M4 in Europe shows all the applique armor added to improve protection over critical areas. The plates on the hull side covered ammunition bins. Note the guards over the periscope covers and the front radio antenna.

M4, 1943 Production, 75mm

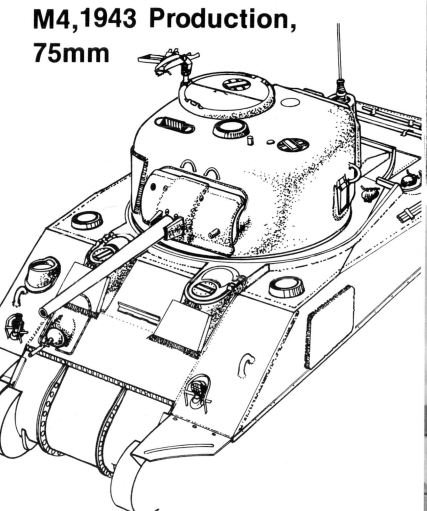

Men of the 36th Infantry Regt., 3rd Armored Division, ride a remanufactured M4 near Stolberg, Germany, October 1944. The sandbag "soft" armor was adopted for more protection against German antitank grenades. Note the mounting girders on the transmission — probably left over from a Cullin Hedgerow Device.

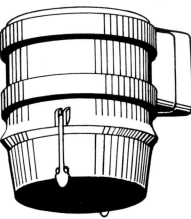

This M4 is covering the advance of the M10 tank destroyer in the background. These vehicles are in Aachen, Germany in October 1944. In the rear stowage are boxes of field rations, rolled tarpaulins and blankets. This vehicle is not camouflaged, but simply shows the effects of weathering and sloppy refueling.

M4 tanks move through Brouvelierures, France, 29 October 1944. This tank has the round air cleaners and applique armor. It has a similar circle and star insignia on the rear plate as the more distant tank, but in this case almost completely painted out.

"Round Type" Air Cleaner

This front view of M4s on Bougainville shows the added frontal armor and M34A1 mantlet of the midwar production version. Note the periscopes in front of the hull hatches, one piece transmission cover, and added gun travel lock.

An M4 of the 68th Tank Battalion, 6th Armored Division, seen in Luxembourg, near Heinerscheid, February 1945. The snow camouflage has been coated with mud on all the front surfaces. The stowage of supplies on the glacis plate was a common practice.

A lineup of M4's — and one M4A1 — of the 749th Tank Btln., attached to the 79th Infantry Division. The lead vehicle is an early M4 with direct vision blots which has been remanufactured with an M34A1 mount and applique armor. An interesting detail is the cable welded to the edge of the hull — this was used to hang stowed items, camouflage nets, etc.

Drive Sprocket Variation

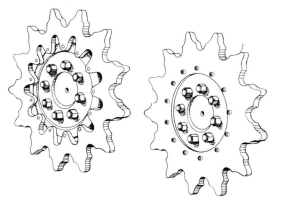

This M4 passes through Dreux, France in August 1944. Note the larger air recognition star on the engine deck. The rear towing pintle has been removed, and the number "119" is painted on the turret. The abandoned German gun is a 7.5 cm PAK 40.

A lineup of Shermans from the 749th Tank Battalion, 7th Army, seen in Embermenil, France, 17 November 1944. The second vehicle from the right is an M4A1, all the others are M4's, Since the M4A1 was mechanically similar to the M4, these two types were occasionally found in one unit. Note the difference in air cleaners, details and stowage.

VVSS
[Vertical
Volume
Spring
Suspension]

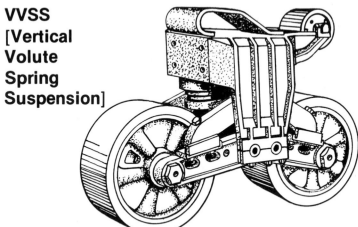

"INK SPOTS", the only original tank left in "I" Company, 32nd Armored Regiment, 3rd Armored Division, fires on German positions near Vicht, Germany, 17 November 1944. The large pile of discarded ammo tubes indicates that like many U.S. tanks, this vehicle is being used as mobile artillery, firing from a prepared position.

[Above] M4's of the 40th Tank Battalion, 7th Armored Division fire on German units near St. Vith, Belgium, during the Battle of the Bulge. The nearest vehicle has camouflage netting draped over the snow-camouflaged hull to soften the hull contours somewhat.

[Below] A graphic example of why many U.S. crews removed the stars from their tanks. The M4 was knocked out by German tanks near Bastogne, Belgium, December 1944. The recovery vehicle is an M26 "Dragon Wagon". It is probable that this tank will be rebuilt for further use, as it does not appear to have burned.

This M4 firing at German snipers across the Marne River is from the same unit as the tanks below. The foliage is attached to camouflage netting hung from the vehicle.

A foliage-draped M4 covers a bridge on the Marne River as infantry run to avoid German sniper fire, August 1944. Under the branches, the engine deck is piled high with extra stowage.

M4A1 Characteristics

The M4A1, the second model to be standardized, was actually the first variant to enter production, the first example being delivered in February 1942, though series deliveries didn't start until March. Three manufacturers built a total of 6,281 M4A1 (75mm) up to January 1944.

In common with the M4, the M4A1 used the Wright R-975 "Whirlwind" aircraft engine, and the other mechanical details were similar. The major difference was in the use of a large one-piece casting for the entire upper hull superstructure. At the time, these hulls were the largest one-piece armor castings ever made. Armor thickness was the same as for the welded hull, and measured 2" in front at an effective angle of inclination of 60°; 1½" on the sides and rear; and 1" on top. The lower hull sides and rear were 1½". The cast turret had 3" of front armor with 2" sides and rear, and 1" roof armor. A small turret side hatch was provided for the loader, intended for discarding spent shell cases. A round ventilator was located on the forward turret roof, and the M34 gun mount was fitted as in the M4.

The hull had direct vision slots and visors in front of the hull hatches, a ventilator to the right of the assistant driver, the 3-piece transmission housing, and a rear deck nearly identical in layout to the M4. The hull rear plate was identical to that of the M4 and both types of air cleaners were used. The very earliest M4A1s had the air cleaners and exhaust layout of the M3 medium. Early M4A1s also had the M3 pattern bogies, and in this form - with full sandshields - the M4A1 first saw combat with the 1st Armoured Division of the British 8th Army at Alamein in October 1942. The British named the M4 the "General Sherman" and "Sherman" was the name which rapidly came to identify all the variants of the M4 family.

Ironically, the M4A1s which fought at Alamein had originally been issued to the U.S. 1st Armored Division at Fort Knox. When the first shipment of M4A1s to Egypt were sunk enroute, the 1st Armored gave up its brand new M4A1s as replacements. Thus, the 1st Armored fought in Tunisia equipped with a mix of older M3 Lees and M4A1 Shermans. The heavy losses at Kasserine Pass were largely the result of inexperience in American armored units - the hard lessons learned by the British in the Western Desert were now learned again in the hills of Tunisia. Faults and weaknesses in the vehicles were assessed and analyzed and corrective action taken. After the victory in North Africa, the M3 medium was withdrawn from front line service, and the M4 family became the sole U.S. medium tank in service.

Improvements to the M4A1 followed the pattern set by the M4. One-piece transmission housings, M4 bogies with larger springs and trailing return rollers, M34A1 gun mounts, elimination of direct vision slots, introduction of applique armor and alternate tracks - all made their appearance in the M4A1 by the middle of 1943. However, a number of early production vehicles in virtually the original North African configuration served to the end of hostilities, especially in Italy, where the terrain and nature of fighting did not make such old vehicles as great a liability as in the Northern European campaign.

Several thousand older Shermans, among them many M4A1s were remanufactured in the United States and England, and upgraded for the European campaign. Applique armor, M34A1 mantlets, and other mechanical

and technical improvements were made, and deliveries from U.S. factories and depots totaled 5,880, including 1,610 M4A3s reworked in Canada. Many more were reworked in England, largely prior to D-Day. With the M4 and M4A3, the M4A1 was one of the most important U.S. service versions of the Sherman and served on all fronts - Europe, Italy, and the Pacific.

Early M4A1, 75mm

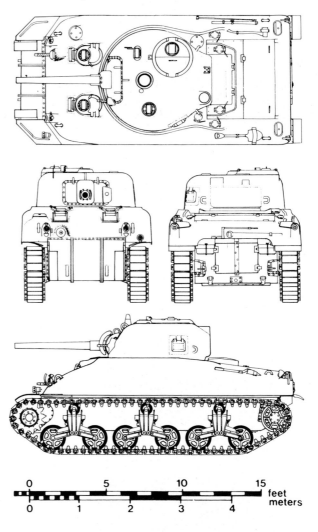

1:76 th scale (4 mm:1 foot)

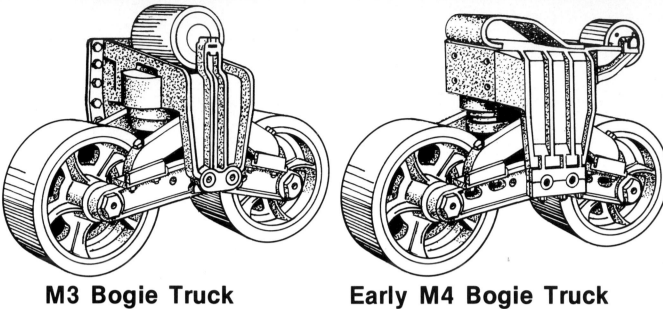

M3 Bogie Truck

Early M4 Bogie Truck

This M4A1 of the 13th Armored Regiment, 1st Armored Division, was photographed at Kasserine Pass, Tunisia, 24 February 1943. The overall scheme is dusty Olive Drab with yellow band, star, and unit ID marking on the turret.

An early production M4A1 lands on a Sicilian beach, 10 July 1943. This vehicle is interesting in that it retains the M3 bogies but has the later driver's positions without direct vision slots. Again, a large pile of soft stowage is tied to the engine deck. This vehicle has been camouflaged in Sand and Olive Drab, the WD number on the rear quarter being in Blue Drab.

One of the first tanks to enter Gela, Sicily, this M4A1 is overall O.D. The crewman in front wears the tanker's coverall and the early tanker's helmet.

Early M4A1, 75mm

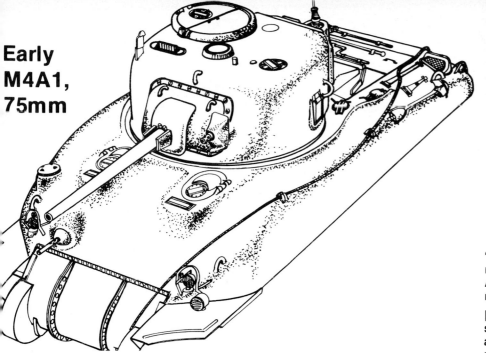

"HANG IT N" sports an old beach umbrella to protect its commander from the rain. This early M4A1 was in the 751st Tank Battalion, attached to the 5th Army, and was photographed near Porretta, Italy, on 6 December 1944, with no modifications.

[Left] Another early M4A1 of the 13th Armored Regt., 1st Armored Division, seen near Anzio, 27 April 1944. Many of these early vehicles went into Italy, as this was the major campaign area. Many of them were never rebuilt or modified in service.

"WEENIE ONE", an extensively camouflaged M4A1 of the 1st Armored Division, seen near Le Ferriere, Italy in late March 1944. This tank retains the M34 mantlet, but has a new fixed turret roof sight replacing the older vertical blade, which has been bent over to clear the new sight. The turret star has been completely overpainted.

VVSS Track

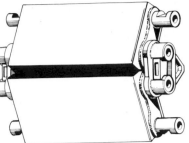

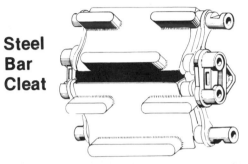

Rubber Block

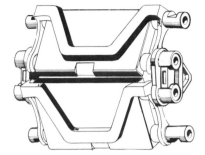

Rubber Chevron

Steel Bar Cleat

Steel Chevron

A line of M4A1's near Turo, Italy on 12 May 1944. These tanks, in the 760th Tank Battalion, show the details of the mid-production 75mm M4A1's. Note the applique armor on the turret to protect the gunner, and the armor shield fastened to the coaxial MG, to protect the exposed slot in the mantlet. The white strips along the road marked the areas cleared of enemy mines. The driver's hatch has no periscope fitted, but the bow gunner's hatch does.

A mixed force of M4A1's and M18 tank destroyers of the 752nd Tank Battalion halts on a road near a forward O.P. overlooking German positions. Independent tank battalions, attached to infantry divisions, or to Corps or Army headquarters, had tank destroyers as a normal part of their establishment. Also, many tank destroyer battalions had tanks in their organization.

An M4A1 with the M34A1 gun mount and full-width mantlet on the Kamiri airstrip, Noemfoor Island, Western New Guinea, moves past the smashed wreck of a Japanese Ki-43 "Oscar". The LVT at the left mounts a 37mm gun, originally designed for the P-39 "Airacobra" and later adopted for PT boats and Amtracs.

This M4A1 of the 191st Tank Btln., crosses the Moselle River, near Arches, France, 22 September 1944, to support troops of the 179th Inf. Regt., 45th Infantry Division. Note how the extra stowage on the engine deck has been carefully aranged and securely tied down to the tank.

M4A1 Rear Deck

Tanks of the 13th Armored Regt., 1st Armored Division, move to a bivouac area in the Anzio beachhead, 27 April 1944. These M4A1's have the round air cleaners and show the locking strap which secured the rear engine access doors. They also demonstrate the common practice of adding extra stowage brackets, racks, etc. to stow extra gear and supplies.

US Tanker, ETO

Two M4A1's of the 1st Armored Division park in a camouflaged bivouac encompment at Anzio, 20 May 1944. The camouflage netting made long range visual identification difficult. Though the tanks are dug-in, they can be backed out of the pits as soon as necessary. Note the extra armor plates added behind the air cleaners.

M4A1's support infantry up Pancake Hill, Hollandia, New Guinea, 22 April 1944. The troops are wearing full assault harnesses and jungle uniforms. These Shermans have the later M34A1 full width mantlets, but no applique armor. Note the steel bar cleat tracks.

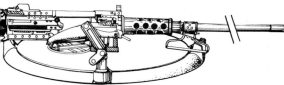

Commander's Gun-Ring Hatch

This tank of the 1st Tank Btln., 1st Armored Division, crosses the Arno River near Casoina, Italy, September 1944. The crew has used spare steel bar cleat track lengths for increased frontal armor. The vehicle is overall very dusty O.D. Note that the right headlight and guard assembly has been removed.

"SLOPPY JOE", of the 603rd Light Tank Company, is seen in Lorengau, Manus Island, In the Admiralty Group, 24 March 1944. This tank destroyed an AT gun, a radio station, and 22 Japanese pillboxes during the Admiralty campaign. Note how the roadwheels have filled with mud.

Late M4A1, 75mm

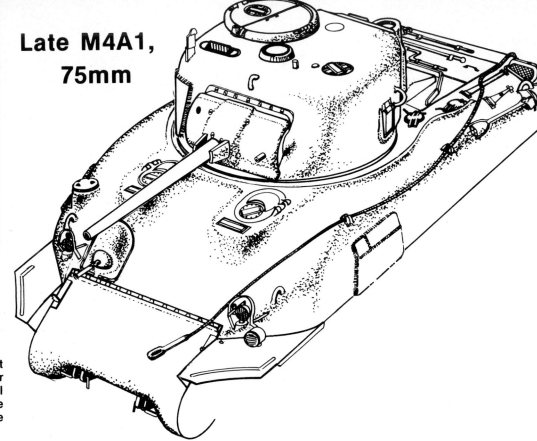

An M4A1 of the 31st Tank Btln., 7th Armored Division, seen near Chartres, France, on 16 August 1944. This vehicle carries the full standard markings, all applique armor and one of the many variations of the Cullin Hedgerow Device. The name was a unit ID practice, and all the tanks would have names beginning with the company letter — here it is a "B" company.

These M4A1's of the 7th Infantry Division on Ebeye Island represent later production 75mm vehicles. They now have full hull applique armor — though none on the turret — and have the M34A1 full width external mantlet, gun travel lock, and later turret roof fixed sight. All of these vehicles have been fitted with grouser bars on the tracks to improve traction in soft terrain.

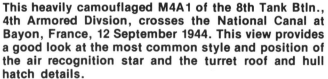

This heavily camouflaged M4A1 of the 8th Tank Btln., 4th Armored Divsion, crosses the National Canal at Bayon, France, 12 September 1944. This view provides a good look at the most common style and position of the air recognition star and the turret roof and hull hatch details.

[Above Right] A burned-out M4A1 is loaded onto an M25 "Dragon Wagon" tank transporter. Most completely burned-out tanks like this one were scrapped, as the heat of an extensive fire usually destroyed the protective quality of the armor.

Two M4A1's, followed by an M4, enter Livorno, Italy, 19 July 1944. These vehicles belonged to a tank battalion supporting the 34th Infantry Division. This shot is a good example of the fact that M4's and M4A1's were operated by the same unit, as they were identical mechanically, having the same engine and power train installation. Note the use of different tracks, there was relatively little standardization in this area.

An M4A1 supporting the 30th Infantry Division passes two wrecked PzKpfw IV ausfJ's, between the St. Fromond bridgehead and St. Lo, France, 9 July 1944. The PzKpfw IV's were from 2nd SS Pz Div. "Das Reich". The M4A1 is the later production model with hull and turret applique armor. Next to the "30 ton" bridging plate is the stencilled shipping instructions.

Late M4A1, 75mm

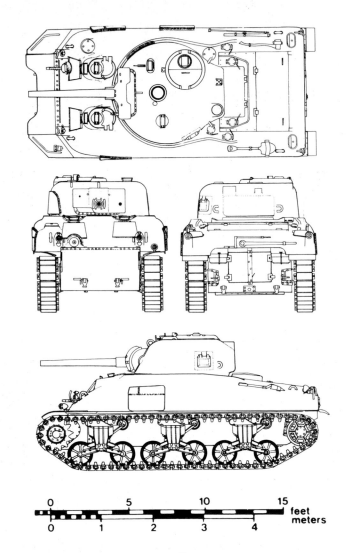

1:76 th scale (4 mm:1 foot)

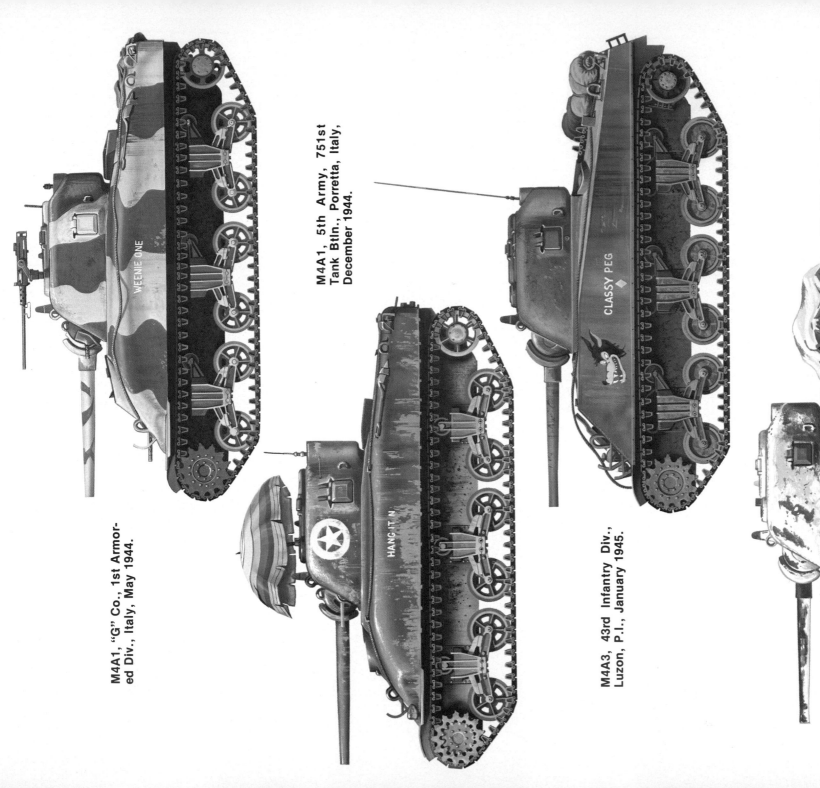

M4A1, "G" Co., 1st Armored Div., Italy, May 1944.

M4A1, 5th Army, 751st Tank Btln., Porretta, Italy, December 1944.

M4A3, 43rd Infantry Div., Luzon, P.I., January 1945.

M4, 7th Armored Div., 40th Tank Btln., St. Vith, Belgium, January 1945.

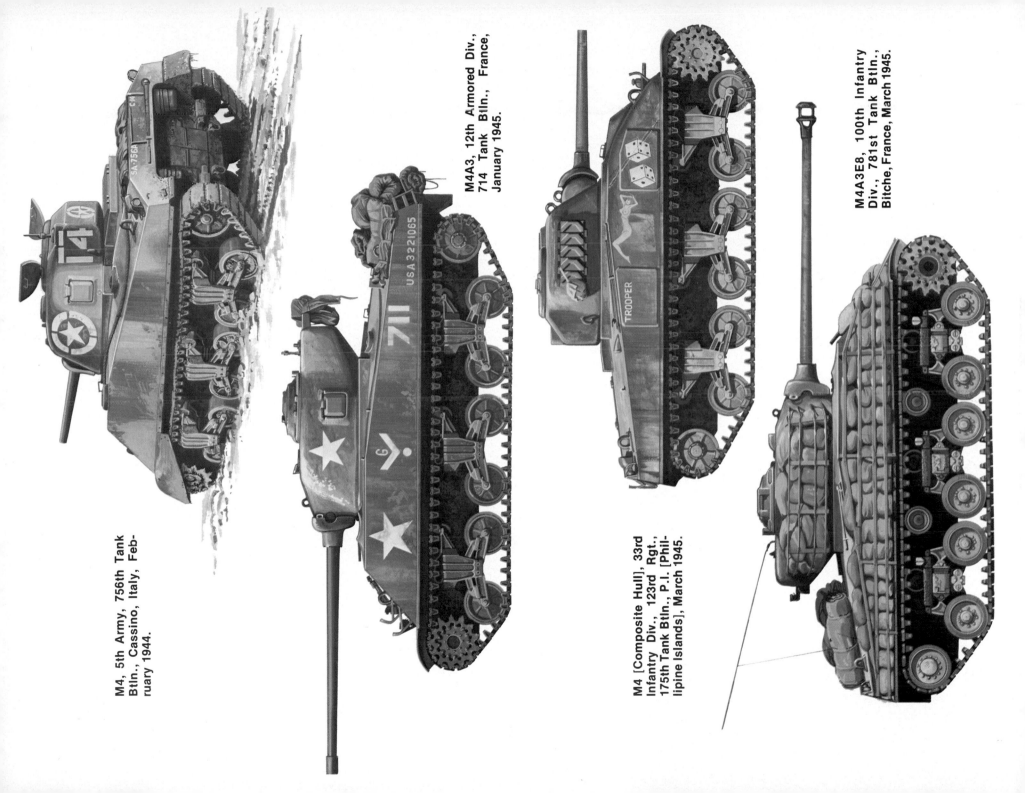

M4, 5th Army, 756th Tank Btln., Cassino, Italy, February 1944.

M4A3, 12th Armored Div., 714 Tank Btln., France, January 1945.

M4 [Composite Hull], 33rd Infantry Div., 123rd Rgt., 175th Tank Btln., P.I. [Phillipine Islands], March 1945.

M4A3E8, 100th Infantry Div., 781st Tank Btln., Bitche, France, March 1945.

M4A3 Characteristics

Early M4A3s had M34 mantlets and direct vision slots for the hull positions, but all M4A3s were built with one-piece cast transmission housings and M4 pattern bogies with track support skids and trailing return rollers. As production continued, the improvements introduced on the other versions were applied to the M4A3: elimination of direct vision slots, M34A1 full width external mantlet mount, applique armor, and various alternate types of tracks. In addition, on all later Shermans, details were improved or altered. Wire cages were provided to protect the periscopes, and other mechanical improvements were made. In common with the M4 and M4A1, many early M4A3s were reworked with applique armor and new mantlets. Whenever it was possible to do so, armored units attempted to use only tanks that were all mechanically similar. Thus, while mixes of M4 and M4A1 versions were not uncommon - because the power train was of the same design - it was usual for M4A3s to be segregated into all M4A3 units. Occasionally, a unit would change from one model to another and then different versions would be seen together, but this brought maintenance problems in the supply of spare parts, manuals, etc.

The M4A3 shared with other Shermans an unsatisfactory ammunition stowage arrangement. The conventional open racks, though protected by the external side armor, were exposed on the inside and ammunition fires were fairly common if the hull or turret were penetrated. Since the standard German PzGr APC projectiles had an explosive filler, nearly every penetration was followed by an explosion or fire. A series of controlled tests by the Ordnance Dept. proved that the major source of tank fires was the ignition of stowed ammunition followed by crew stowage, interior stores of lubricants for maintenance, and lastly the fuel tanks in the rear. Many tanks burned fiercely, even with empty fuel tanks. The result was the development of wet stowage for the revised hulls introduced in 1944. An interim solution was the fitting of 1" applique armor over the three most exposed ammunition bins, and over the front faces of the hull hatch box extensions, which being nearly vertical were more easily penetrated than the 60° inclined glacis plate. Even such improvements did not always prove effective. Many U.S. tank crews - sometimes encouraged or ordered to do so - crammed their M4s full of as much ammo as they could stuff into every available nook and cranny. The best protected ammo bins were of no use if any loose rounds caught fire. One 3rd Armored Division veteran described how his M4, "loaded to the rafters" with HE and WP (white phosphorus), took a hit under the mantlet from the PzKpfw IV hidden in a store in a French village and blew up in a matter of seconds, providing an interesting photo for the divisional history showing the turret lying in the street a good distance away from the hull. Except for the loader, everyone got out, but it was close. "INK SPOTS", the M4 seen on page 12, was in the same company as the blown-up M4 described. Note the huge pile of shell tubes and the fresh ammo piled on the engine deck, some 4 months after the earlier incident. This questionable practice continued through the end of the war.

The M4A3 was the major U.S. service variant of the Sherman series, and was the model chosen to be retained postwar. With a welded hull virtually identical to that of the M4 except for the engine deck and hull rear details, the

M4A3 was powered by the Ford GAA V-8 tank engine, which originally had been designed as a 12-cylinder aircraft engine. Two manufacturers built 1,690 M4A3 (75mm, Dry) with the original 60° glacis hull. Another 3,071 M4A3 (75mm, Wet) were constructed with revised ammunition stowage in a redesigned hull. Overall, in all versions, the M4A3 was built in much greater numbers than any other Sherman model. Though the more compact V-8 engine and propeller shaft arrangement would have allowed a significant lowering of the Sherman's rather high silhouette, the need to avoid interruption of production prevented adoption of any new designs, and thus the old M4 type hull was retained.

M4A3, 75mm

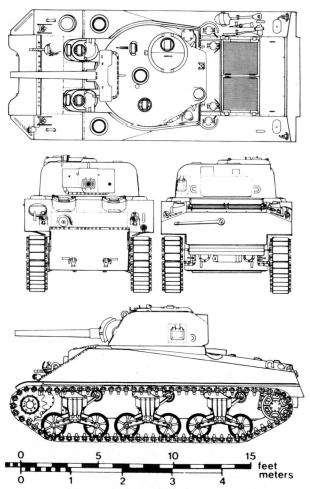

0   5   10   15
feet
meters
0   1   2   3   4

1:76 th scale (4 mm:1 foot)

[Above] Two M4A3's fire on German holdouts in Mulhouse, southern France, 23 November 1944. These tanks do not have any applique armor. Note the empty shell casings between the tanks and the large number of "empties" next to the M7 Priest in the background. These vehicles show one of the primary distinctions from the M4, if the engine deck is not visible, namely the altered shape of the superstructure rear overhang.

[Below] A foliage covered M4A3 passes through the ruins of Coutances, France, 31 July 1944. Allied artillery and air bombardment leveled most of the town.

An M4A3 of the 31st Tank Btln, 7th Armored Division, moves past a German light truck. The foliage is tied to chicken wire which has been fastened to the hull and turret. Note the track support skids on top of the bogie trucks and the solid rear idler and roadwheels.

M4A3 Mid Production,
75mm

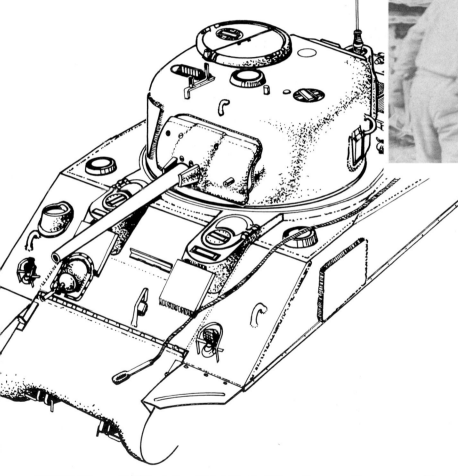

"COZY II", an M4A3 of the 751st Tank Btln., fires on German positions on Mt. Belvedere, Italy, 22 February 1945. This tank is a standard mid-production 75mm M4A3. The roadwheels are the cast open type, but so covered with mud that they appear solid.

Improving the Breed.....

As mentioned, the problems in the early Sherman designs were identified and attempts were made to alleviate or eliminate as many of these flaws as possible, providing that such corrections would not slow the flow of Shermans coming from the 11 major manufacturers who assembled the vehicles. As a result, some problems, like the vertical sides and high hull shape, were never to be corrected because building a completely new hull would have meant halting production while new jigs and tooling were brought onto the line. Yet thousands of minor engineering changes were introduced without seriously affecting production, as was shown by the increasing production achieved during 1942 and 1943.

Many of these changes were those already described - the normal process of improving and modifying a design during production. Others involved progressive changes in materials or design. For example, a different roadwheel design was adopted during the war. The earlier cast 5-spoked industrial wheel with lightening holes being replaced by a stamped 6-spoked solid wheel which appeared early in 1942, becoming more common as the war progressed.

Perhaps the most obvious changes concerned crew hatch arrangements and the stowage of ammunition. Combat reports had indicated that the early hatches were inadequate for emergency exits, especially in the turret. Thus, many of the later production 75mm turrets introduced an oval loader's hatch on the left side of the turret roof. This meant that the loader didn't have to wait for the commander and gunner to leave before he could get out. Very late 75mm turrets had the gun-ring hatch for the commander replaced with a new cupola with 6 fixed armor glass episcopes and a one-piece hatch with a fully rotating periscope for the tank commander. Larger hatches were also designed for the driver and assistant driver and in order to allow these new hatches to be fitted, the front areas of the cast and welded hulls had to be redesigned. On the welded hull, the result was a completely new glacis plate inclined at 47° instead of 60° and presenting a flat surface with no protrusions except for the bow machine gun. The glacis eliminated the weak points formed by the hatch box extensions and the larger hatches were fitted at an angle in the new forward hull roof which extended several inches farther forward than on the older hull. The last production model of the M4 (75mm) was an interesting hybrid in that instead of adopting the all welded 47° glacis hull of the M4A3, it used a composite hull with a welded rear and a cast front end identical to that eventually adopted for the M4A1 with the 76mm gun. The M4 composite was also noteworthy in that it was the only late configuration hull to retain applique armor because it also kept the original dry stowage for its 75mm ammunition.

The new stowage arrangement, used for the M4A3 75mm with the 47° glacis hull, and for all later 76mm Shermans, consisted of new ammunition racks surrounded by hollow jackets filled with a mixture of ethylene glycol antifreeze and water. If a bin was hit by splinters and blast from a shell that penetrated the hull or turret, the liquid jacket would be punctured and, theoretically, put out a fire before it could ignite all the ammunition. The development did not improve the situation, because the frequent stowage of excess ammo defeated the purpose of the new racks, as the extra rounds were unprotected.

Because of the steady increase in weight and varied types of difficult terrain encountered in service, track modifications were developed. Grousers were steel bars with blunt blade edges that could be fastened across the tracks to provide traction in slippery conditions like mud or soft sand. Extended end connectors (sometimes called "duckbills") were attached to the standard track connectors to widen the track 4" to 20½". Because the extended end connectors were not level with the tread, they became effective only after the tracks had sunk part way into soft ground. Extended end connectors saw wide service, especially on later models fitted with VVSS. Very late M4A3 (75mm, Wet) had the new HVSS.

Late M4, 75mm, with Composite Hull

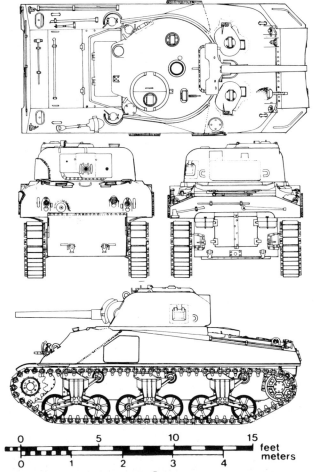

1:76 th scale (4 mm:1 foot)

A composite hull M4, of the 775th Tank Btln., is seen in the Phillipines, June 1945. The 775th was attached to the 37th Infantry Division. The truck is a wrecked Japanese Toyota KB 1½ ton model.

Marine Tank Sgt., Pacific

Late composite hull M4s of the 175th Tank Btln. support the 33rd Infantry Division near Baguio, Luzon, Phillipines, 8 March 1945. The dice on each tank are different and may indicate the units or tank positions in the battalion. these markings must be among the most elaborate ever used to decorate an armored vehicle, each one having a name as well as the dice, and at least two have "cheese cake" nudes in addition.

The center tank, a late M4, was hit by Japanese antitank fire, and the other tanks have surrounded it and are firing at suspected enemy emplacements. This photo was taken on Okinawa, in late June 1945. The nearest tank is an older M4A3 with the 60° glacis, and the tank at the right is a newer M4A3 with the 47° glacis plate hull.

[Right] A composite hull M4 passes through Coutances, France, 31 July 1944. The foliage is intended to conceal the tank from enemy artillery spotters.

[Left] An M4 of the 68th Tank Btln., 6th Armored Division passes through Avranches, France. This is a late M4 with the composite cast/welded hull and full applique armor. Note the air recognition circle and star on the tarp over the rear deck.

This view of a composite hull M4 shows the new cast front end, which was identical to the front hull of the redesigned M4A1. The driver's hatches were enlarged to allow faster exits and to some extent the armor protection was improved. All of these late M4's had hull applique armor as a standard feature. These tanks of the 763rd Tank Btln. were photographed in Leyte, 23 November 1944.

Standard End Connector

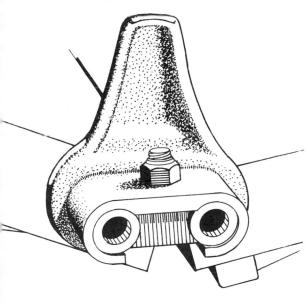

Two composite hull M4's seen from the left side show the standard left applique armor and the joint between the cast nose and welded rear hull. These tanks, seen on Guam in August 1944 both have names beginning with "C", indicated they belong to "C" company of the tank battalion. The first tank is "COGNAC", the second is "CUPID".

This late M4 has been fitted with grousers for extra traction in poor terrain. The grousers extended across the tracks and were attached to the end connectors. This tank has been disabled by a land mine near Dulag, Leyte Island, Phillipine Islands.

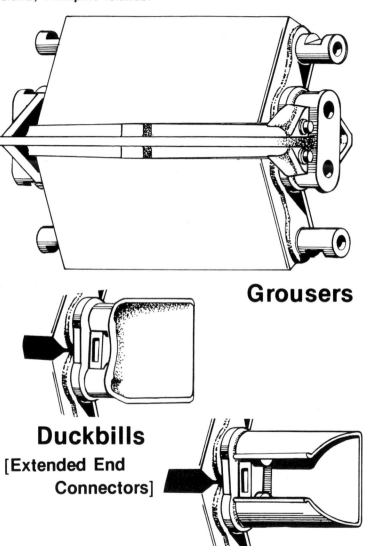

Grousers

Duckbills
[Extended End Connectors]

Composite hull M4's of the 81st Infantry Division, seen on the island of Angaur in the Palau island group, on 20 September 1944. These vehicles use the steel bar cleat type of track and have pressed steel solid wheels. They are from "B" company of the tank battalion.

This burned-out M4A3 on Luzon was destroyed by a 47mm antitank gun, 19 January 1945. It shows the shape and details of the new 47° glacis plate. An unusual detail is the narrow strip of applique armor on the lower forward turret side.

An M4A3 of the 379th Regt., 95th Infantry Division moves down a street in Saarlautern-Roden, Germany, 2 January 1945. This vehicle shows the great variety in markings and stowage practices of American armored units, having complete markings and no "soft" armor.

This M4A3 attached to the 43rd. Infantry Division passes a burning Japanese "Shinhoto Chiha" tank on Luzon in the Phillipines, 17 January 1945. This tank shows the changes made in later production 75mm M4A3's. Note the new hull design with a 47° inclined glacis plate and larger hull hatches, and the oval loader's hatch in the turret roof. The applique armor was no longer needed because the ammunition was now stowed in liquid-protected bins to suppress ammunition fires.

Late M4A3, 75mm, Wet Stowage, Field Modified

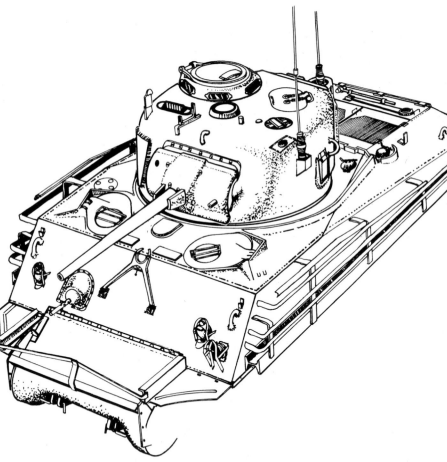

This tank is one of the several firing at German positions in Dombasle, France, 15 September 1944. Another tank has just hit a house suspected of being used as an observation post. Note how the turret star is mostly obscured, a standard practice in many units.

This tank of the 25th Tank Btln., 14th Armored Division, was photographed in Huttendorf, 11 February 1945. Sandbags have been added all around the hull as protection from German antitank rockets. Beneath all the sandbags, this is the later 47° glacis hull.

A tank of the 10th Armored Division sits in the Adolf Hitler Platz in Trier, Germany, 2 March 1945. Part of the paint or mud used to overpaint the white turret star was peeled off. From the side, the new 47° glacis plate is easy to identify. An unusual detail is the liberated civilian shotgun leaning against the rear of the turret.

[Above Left] Another M4A3 of the 25th Tank Btln., 14th Armored Division passes through the rubble that was Oberhoffen, France, 6 February 1945. This tank has a neat layer of sandbags all around the hull, though as yet the turret has not received this protection. As more U.S. tanks had encounters with German antitank rocket weapons, "soft" armo became more common.

This disabled M4A3 of the 43rd Tank Btln., 12th Armored Division, is being repaired with the help of two TRV's. While one recovery vehicle winches the track through the mud, another TRV holds the tank at an angle to raise the bogies for clearance. This photo was taken 11 February 1945.

This front view of the M4A3E2, seen near Langerwehe, Germany, shows the uncluttered glacis characteristic of this model. The cast transmission housing was up to 6" thick and the built up glacis was 4" thick; the headlights were eliminated. This vehicle has the 75mm gun. All M4A3E2's had extended end connectors, as the weight was 10 tons more than a standard M4A3 [76mm].

M4A3E2 "Jumbo" Assault Tank

Because of the vastly greater number of tanks available to the Allies, they did not have to resort to the use of limited traverse weapons like the StuG III or StuH 42. U.S. tank destroyers and 105mm howitzer-armed Shermans performed the same functions as the German StuG's. Nonetheless, in view of armor's role as a supporting force against strongpoints, and with the assault on the much-touted Siegfried Line in mind, attempts were made to produce a heavily armored assault tank capable of absorbing more punishment in breaching enemy fortified positions. The T14 assault tank proved to be unsuccessful, suffering from track and suspension problems, and as an expedient measure, it was decided to add armor to an existing model of the Sherman.

The M4A3 (75mm) with the new 47° glacis hull was chosen, although dry ammunition stowage was retained. The front and sides had 1½" thick plate welded over them, giving a front thickness of 4" and upper hull sides of 3". A new cast transmission housing of 5½" thickness was fitted. The obvious increase in bulk of this modified hull led to the M4A3E2s nickname "Jumbo".

The turret for the 'E2 was a completely new design though obviously influenced by the T23 turret previously adopted for the 76mm Shermans. It was an immensely thick casting having 3" of frontal armor - further protected by a 7" thick block-shaped mantlet - and 6" thick sides. The rear was 2½" thick and the 1" roof plate was welded into the top of the turret casting during assembly, leaving a welding seam around the roof. In view of its role as an assault tank, the M4A3E2 retained the 75mm gun M3, since the 76mm weapon had no advantage in firing HE ammo.

Because of the increased weight - to 42 tons - all M4A3E2s were permanently fitted with extended end connectors. Performance fell from 26 mph maximum road speed to 22 mph and range was reduced. However, the added armor made the 'E2 assault tank extremely resistant to German antitank guns and tanks. PzKpfw IV's had to use their heavily rationed APCR solid shot at all but point-blank range, and even Panthers couldn't penetrate the frontal armor at long range. M4A3E2s eventually became popular for leading armor columns, as they often absorbed hits that would have destroyed the standard Shermans, and gave the other vehicles warning of German antitank guns.

Seen in an ordnance depot in Cherbourg, France, this vehicle is an M4A3E2 assault tank. This special tank was built in limited numbers and featured armor up to 7" thick. This excellent high view shows all of the details of the unique turret of the 'E2. The M4A3E2 was armed with a standard 75mm M3 gun. Note the 7" thick built-up mantlet and the wider turret with sides 6" thick. The 1" roof plate was welded to the cast turret shell.

76mm Shermans

Although official Army doctrine placed the responsibility for destroying enemy armor with the Tank Destroyer Command, the inadequacy of the 75mm M3 gun in engaging enemy tanks had become obvious. In response to pressure from Ordnance and recommendations from units in the field and from the Armored Force, upgunning the Sherman was planned for the beginning of 1944.

Ordnance had originally tested a 76mm high velocity gun in an M4A1 with the original turret in 1942. Ballistic tests were satisfactory, but it was obvious that the old turret was too small and a new turret had to be designed. The T23, an experimental medium tank built in limited numbers, had a larger turret which used the same 69" turret ring. It was distinguished by a longer rear extension and a new flat front mantlet. With suggested changes and improvements, the T23 turret was adopted for all versions of the M4 family to be built with 76mm guns. The M4 was not fitted with the 76mm gun, but was reserved for 105mm howitzer armament. The M4A2 was reserved for Lend-Lease, and thus the M4A1 and M4A3 were the only U.S. service Shermans to mount the 76mm high velocity weapon. Pressed Steel Car Co. built 3,396 M4A1 (76mm, Wet) from January 1944 to June 1945. Apparently no records were kept indicating how many had VVSS and how many received the new HVSS and 23" track, but most vehicles built after August 1944 could have been fitted with the new suspension. Two plants turned out 1,925 M4A3 (76mm, Wet) with VVSS from March 1944 to December 1944.

With the adoption of the 76mm gun and T23 turret, the M4A1 also received the later cast hull with wet stowage, revised front contours, and the larger hull hatches set at an angle. On all the late hulls, the larger hull hatches were hinged to open out and forward to clear the larger T23 turret. Many vehicles received extended end connectors because of a 5% increase in weight with the new gun and turret. The original 76mm M1A1 gun had a bore length of 53 calibers (L/53) and fired the standard APC round at 2,600 fps. Its standard penetration was approximately 1" better than the 75mm M3, about 4". A special tungsten-core APCR shot - reserved for tank destroyers - was capable of penetrating over 6" of armor at 500 yds., and was very effective against most German tanks. It is probable that some 76mm Sherman crews were able to obtain supplies of the "hot" ammunition from TD crews - the M18 "Hellcat" had the same 76mm weapon - or from some supply depots.

The usefulness of the heavily armored M4A3E2 has already been discussed, and in the spring of 1945, its suitability as an expedient "heavy" tank was recognized in an Army field technical order, March 1945, authorizing the rearming of the M4A3E2 with the 76mm gun. This was possible because the 76mm had been designed to use the same trunnions as the 75mm M3. It is not known if such armament conversions had been tried earlier, but as it was possible to do so, it may have been done.

Working from the other direction, Ordnance developed field kits for adding extra armor to the glacis plate of standard Shermans. These were full width one-piece plates 1" thick that covered the complete glacis and the upper part of the cast transmission housing. Some field units had been making their own "up-armoring" kits by cutting apart wrecked tanks and welding the armor pieces to their vehicles. Though designed for the welded hull M4A3s, these armor kits were often applied to M4A1s, the "spaced" armor effect proving effective in breaking up enemy AP projectiles.

With the increased contact with the newer German hollow-charge antitank rocket weapons (the 8.8cm Raketenpanzerbüchse [bazooka] and "Panzerfaust" AT grenade), U.S. crews in many units adopted "soft" armor to prevent these weapons from detonating against the hull or turret armor. Though wood and spaced spare tracks were used, the most common expedient appears to have been the use of sandbags, often carried in very elaborate, if crudely made, framework which supported the sandbags all around the hull and sometimes the turret. The sandbags appear to have been effective against the antitank rocket weapons and were in widespread use by the end of the war.

M4A1, 76mm

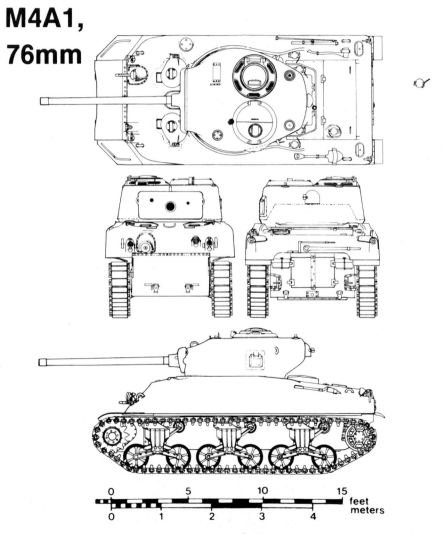

0 5 10 15 feet
0 1 2 3 4 meters

1:76 th scale (4 mm:1 foot)

An M4A1 of the 66th Armored Regiment, 2nd Armored Division, passes through Aubencheil-Aubac, France, September 1944. In this view, the new M4A1 hull seems to be the same as the earlier model. Only the larger hatches canted at an angle positively identify the new hull. However, all late M4A1's were built with the 76mm gun in the T23 turret, another recognition feature.

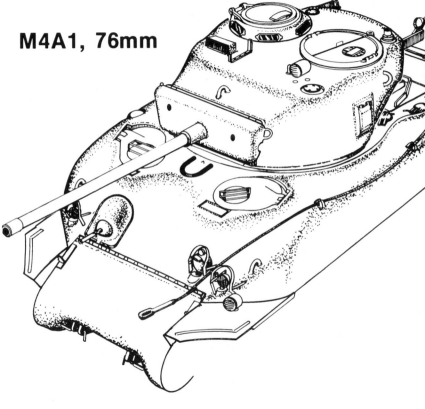

M4A1, 76mm

A 76mm M4A1 with a Cullin Hedgerow Device passes through a break in a hedgerow cleared by Army engineer bulldozers. This tank was in the 3rd Armored Division, photographed on 26 July 1944. A second color, probably field drab [brown] has been used on the hull.

An M4A1 of the 67th Armored Regiment, 2nd Armored Division, enters the French village of St. Sever Calvados, 3 August 1944. Note the large air recognition circle and star painted on the turret roof.

[Above Right] This M4A1 [76mm] of the 3rd Armored Division, 1st Army, was photographed near Korbach, Germany, 30 March 1945. A very unusual fitting is the use of two 1" thick armor plate kits to add protection in front. These field modification kits were designed for the later 47° welded hull front, and as can be seen, were intended to partially cover the transmission housing as well. The frontal armor on this tank is about 4½" thick. However, the strangest detail is that the commander's cupola and loader's gun-ring hatch have been transposed on the turret roof: the loader's ring hatch on the right and the C.O.'s cupola on the left!

This camouflaged M4A1 [76mm] shows the larger hull hatches and 76mm M1 gun. This tank has rubber-chevron block track [the chevrons are nearly worn off] with extended end connectors. As was common in Europe, this group of tanks of the 2nd Armored Division, are carrying infantry toward their objective in Belgium, 27 December 1944. The troops are from the 291st Inf. Regt., 75th Infantry Division.

This M4A3 [76mm] passes through Benwihr, Belgium, 27 December 1944. With the white star and ring on the turret painted out, this vehicle presents the drab appearance common in U.S. armored units in the later stages of the European campaign.

M4A3, 76mm

There were several possible variations in fittings and details on the M4A3 (76mm). The T23 turret originally was built with a new cupola for the commander and the old gun ring hatch was moved to the left for use as the loader's hatch. It retained the .50 Browning HMG for antiaircraft use. As production got under way, the gun ring hatch was replaced by the smaller oval loader's hatch introduced on the very late 75mm gun turret. The .50 MG was moved to a fixed stanchion mount on the turret centerline near the rear of the loader's hatch. The oval loader's hatch did not block vision from the commander's cupola episcopes when it was fully open, and it provided slightly more room in the turret as there were no internal fittings for the oval hatch. Stowage for the .50 Browning was sometimes provided on the rear of the turret. When stowed, the pintle was set into a socket on the rear-mounted turret ventilator and the barrel jacket clamped in a circular bracket on the left rear corner of the turret. Usually the barrel was removed and stowed between the two rear brackets, and the gun and barrel were fitted with canvas covers.

The M1A1 gun was modified and improved, and later versions were fixed with a double-baffle muzzle brake very similar to the common German pattern. Such was the speed and extent of production of the M4A3, that there were significant overlaps of details. One factory began producing HVSS-equipped vehicles in August 1944 while the second plant continued making VVSS fitted M4A3's through December 1944. Thus, occasionally, VVSS M4A3 (76mm) may be seen with the later turret with the oval loader's hatch and M1A1C or M1A2 gun with muzzle brake, while early HVSS models had the gun-ring hatch and no muzzle brake. Crew or unit modifications also altered the appearance of many vehicles, and external stowage arrangements tended to be more extensive than on earlier models.

Two vehicles of the 747th Med. Tank Battalion show difference in added armor. Steel track sections were welded to the turret sides and hull sides of the M4A3 on the right, and to the glacis plates of both vehicles, adding 2" of armor. Sandbags were fastened over the added "armor", and open 4" grid metal mesh with cheesecloth netting covers the sandbags.

[Below Right] This M4A3 [76mm] of the 1st Armored Division is seen after returning from firing practice. It carries the standard unit marking stencilling, plus a large air ID star on the engine deck. Note the overhang of the T23 turret, the new cupola with armor glass episcopes and the canvas-covered .50 Browning MG stowed in brackets on the turret.

An M4A3 [76mm] of the 5th Army in the Po River area of Italy, 26 April 1945, provides an excellent view of the standard late model M4A3. This vehicle has an oval loader's hatch in the turret roof. Note the tarpaulin over the stowed items on the engine deck, and the grousers fastened to the side of the turret. The hull stencilling denotes the depot that processed the vehicle after shipment from the U.S. Often, such markings remained on a tank for some time. This is one of the few 76mm Shermans with the muzzle brake to see action. Note the scavenged licence plate attached to the gun travel lock.

Infantry of the 2nd Inf. Division board tanks of the 741st Tank Btln., attached to the 9th Inf. Regt. of the division, 30 March 1945. All these tanks have extended end connectors and added grab rails along the hull sides to enable infantry to board the vehicles more easily.

Troops of the 1st Infantry Division take cover behind supporting M4A3 tanks in St. Andreasburg, Germany, as snipers fire from undetected locations. The vehicle at the left is an M4A3E8 with HVSS and the later 23" steel chevron track. The VVSS M4A3 [76mm] in the center shows the usual drab appearance of late war U.S. armor. Note the broken extended end connectors; these were easily sheared off or bent by driving too close to curbs or roadside obstructions.

An M4A3 [76mm] of the 629th Tank Destroyer Btln. fires between houses in Gurzenich, Germany to locate hidden German emplacements, 14 December 1944. On the left side of the engine deck are stowed a roadwheel and a spare volute spring. Note the rear grill, intended to direct air and exhaust straight to the rear to reduce the amount of dust raised by the vehicle. Racks on either side of the rear overhang hold replacement rubber blocks for track repair.

Rear of T23 turret

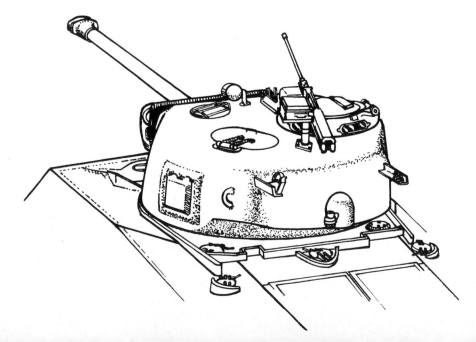

Vehicles of a tank battalion attached to the 5th Army wait in Bonizzo, Italy for a pontoon bridge to be completed across the Po River, 25 April 1945. The nearest row of vehicles are M4A3 [76mm] tanks; behind them are M18 Hellcat tank destroyers and M20 scout cars. Again, most of the Shermans carry no significant markings.

An M4A3 of the 774th Tank Btln. passes a knocked-out Panther ausf G on a forest road near Bovigny, Belgium, 17 January 1945. The 774th was an independent tank battalion attached to Gen. George Patton's 3rd Army.

M4A3E8, 76mm, HVSS

One of the advantages of the early Vertical Volute Spring Suspension (VVSS) was that the design did not occupy any space inside the hull. Also, it was developed and available when production of medium tanks was expanded tremendously. There were, however, severe disadvantages: a rough ride, excessive ground pressure with the heavier models, and the need to jack up the tank itself in order to change a damaged roadwheel - the bogie had to be lifted above the tracks so the wheel could clear the guide teeth. Extended end connectors improved the ground pressure problem, but they could be damaged by hitting rocks or obstructions - running too close to a raised curb could break off all the extended connectors at one time.

Ordnance had tested many experimental suspension and track designs to replace VVSS and the 16½" double-pin track. The most successful was a developed form of Horizontal Volute Spring Suspension (HVSS) which featured 4 wheels per bogie with the bogie frame in the center. Thus, changing a wheel required jacking up only one end of a bogie frame to slide the wheel out over the track. Inboard wheels were removed under the hull. New wider tracks using center guide teeth were developed, and two designs were used on WWII Shermans with HVSS. The first was the T66 single dry pin, 23" wide steel track recognized by its solid one-piece links and scalloped leading edge contour. This was the track used on the earlier HVSS vehicles. The T80 was a double-pin 23" track with split track shoes, using end connectors as for the old 16½" track with separate center guide connectors carrying the guide teeth. It was

standardized for postwar use, variations and later developments of which are in use today on modern U.S. tanks.

The new track and HVSS provided a much improved ride and better flotation in soft ground, and most of the Shermans retained for postwar use had HVSS. The M4A3 (76mm, Wet) HVSS - to use its official Ordnance designation - had been designated M4A3E8 in the test phase, and it became known as the "Easy Eight" when being distinguished from the VVSS models. Until postwar modifications in other countries, the 'E8 represented the culmination of 3 years of development of the M4 series and was the last of the line of combat tanks called "Sherman".

M4A3E8, 76mm, HVSS

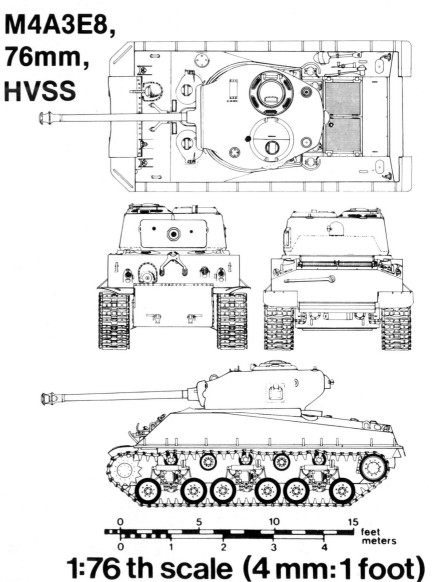

This front view of an M4A3E8 of the 21st Tank Btln., 10th Armored Division, shows the original T66 single-pin 23" track used with the new HVSS chassis. The wider track and horizontal volute spring suspension provided better flotation in rough terrain and a much smoother ride. The turret .50 HMG has a full 100 round box.

1:76 th scale (4 mm:1 foot)

This interesting shot of tanks of the 4th Armored Division, 3rd Army was taken in Alzey, Germany 20 March 1945. The vehicle on the right is an M4A3E8 with HVSS and T66 track. It is the tank used by the commander of the 37th Tank Btln. of the 4th Armored. The Vehicle on the left is an M4A3E2 assault tank, rearmed with the 76mm gun, as authorized by a U.S. Army field order in March 1945.

HVSS
[Horizontal Volute Spring Suspension]

This early M4A3E8 of the 41st Tank Btln., 11th Armored Division, 3rd Army, was the first vehicle in the unit to reach the Rhine River, 21 March 1945. This tank has the gun ring hatch for the loader, T66 single-pin track, and extra welded armor on the glacis. The added armor has been pieced together from 1" armor plate. In many cases, wrecked tanks, Allied and German, were cut apart to provide additional armor for this purpose.